ALBÉNIZ

ESPAÑA OPUS 165 FOR THE PIANO

Six Album Leaves

G000116119

EDITED BY OLGA LLANO KUEHL-WHITE

CONTENTS

About the Composer 1

About the Music 3

Performance Suggestions 3

About This Edition 4

Editorial Considerations 5

Glossary of Spanish Terms 5

ESPAÑA: SIX ALBUM LEAVES, OP. 165

No. 1, Prélude 6

No. 2, Tango 10

No. 3, Malagueña 13

No. 4, Serenata 20

No. 5, Capricho Catalán 26

No. 6, Zortzico 32

About the Composer

The music of Isaac Albéniz mirrors his life—both are colorful and passionate. For over 100 years, biographical information on Albéniz has included several falsehoods, including stories that he stowed away on ships, and that he studied with Liszt. Albéniz himself often gave exaggerated facts to embellish his career, even though in reality he led a very charmed life. As a brilliant pianist, he toured successfully and extensively in his country and abroad. In the last two decades of his life, his interest turned more intensively to composition of operas, zarzuelas, vocal music, and music for piano. As one of Spain's most outstanding musicians, his works for piano—especially those in a Spanish idiom—are indisputably his lasting legacy.

Isaac Manuel Francisco Albéniz y Pascual was born in Camprodón, Province of Gerona, in Catalonia, Spain on May 29, 1860. As a child prodigy, he was introduced to the piano by his talented sister Clementina. At age 8, he entered the Real Conservatorio in Madrid, and by age 12, he was performing throughout Spain. When his father—a customs official—temporarily accepted a government position in Cuba, Albéniz gave performances in Havana and Puerto Rico.

Returning to Spain, Albéniz and his mother traveled to Germany where he studied briefly at the Leipzig Hochschule für Musik, followed by three years at the Conservatoire Royal in Brussels, the latter financed by Count Guillermo Morphy, secretary to King Alfonso XII. Albéniz soon began playing

This volume is dedicated to the memory of Alicia de Larrocha, who was my teacher, mentor, and dear friend.

—*Olga Llano Kuehl-White*

Cover art: Market Day in Spain, *1877*
by Filippo Baratti (Italian, fl.1877–1901)
Private Collection / Photo © Bonhams, London, UK
The Bridgeman Art Library

concerts extensively and with great success. In 1880, he traveled to Vienna, Prague and Budapest, where he had hoped to study with Franz Liszt (1811–1886), only to find him away on tour. Not wanting to disappoint his father who had subsidized the trip, Albéniz himself concocted the story about studying with the great musician.

At the age of 23, he moved to Barcelona and married one of his students, Rosita Jordana Lagarriga (1863–1945). Around the same time, he met Felipe Pedrell (1841–1922), a teacher, musicologist and opera composer. Pedrell was a strong advocate of Spanish Nationalism and provided the creative impetus that Albéniz needed, encouraging him and other composers to utilize the musical elements of Spain's folk songs and dances. Albéniz was especially drawn to flamenco, the exotic music of Andalucía, and this was his inspiration for many of his finest works for piano.

At the Exposición Universal in Barcelona in 1888, representatives of the Erard piano manufacturing company heard Albéniz perform, and invited him to give a concert in Paris the following year. The concert was attended by composers Gabriel Fauré (1845–1924), Claude Debussy (1862–1918), Maurice Ravel (1875–1937) and Paul Dukas (1865–1935). That same year, Albéniz performed several concerts in London, receiving critical acclaim.

Although an ardent Spaniard proud of his heritage, Albéniz recognized that the Spanish political and cultural environment was not as conducive for musicians as was Paris or London, so in 1890 he purchased a home in Brompton, England for his wife and three children. Until the age of 30, Albéniz toured extensively, turning more towards composition during the last two decades of his life. Around 1893, his manager Henry Lowenfeld introduced him to Francis Money-Coutts (1852–1923) a poet, librettist and wealthy heir of the Coutts banking family. Money-Coutts supported Albéniz in return for the composer setting his poetry and librettos to music. Their best collaboration was the opera *Pepita Jimenez*, which was based on a novel by Juan

Valera (1824–1905). It was performed in Italian, which was the custom of the time, and premiered in Barcelona in 1896. Many years later, it was translated into Spanish and revised as an opera in three acts by composer Pablo Sorozábal (1897–1988), premiering in Madrid's Teatro de Zarzuela in 1964.

During his years in England, Albéniz continued to perform throughout Europe both as a soloist and with various orchestras, and also performed a great deal of chamber music in Barcelona. However, many musicians urged him to return to France. Albéniz's wife also preferred Paris since she was more fluent in French than in English. The family moved to Paris in 1894, and their home became a gathering place for writers, musicians and artists. While in Paris, Albéniz taught piano at the Schola Cantorum where he also studied counterpoint with Vincent d'Indy (1851–1931) and met French composers Erik Satie (1866–1925), Albert Roussel (1869–1937) and Déodat de Séverac (1872–1921). He had the opportunity to attend premiers of Debussy's works and developed close friendships with both Fauré and Dukas. French influences are very evident in his final masterwork, *Iberia*.

Around 1898, Albéniz suffered serious health problems, and his failing kidneys were of grave concern. In 1905, he began work on his immortal masterpiece, *Iberia*, a collection of 12 pieces for piano, evoking Spanish scenes and places. With a new, enriched harmonic vocabulary, *Iberia* brought Spanish music into the 20th century.

By 1908, Albéniz's rapidly declining health caused the family to leave Paris in search of cures or restoratives. Many friends visited regularly, and composer Enrique Granados (1867–1916) presented him with a letter from Debussy informing Albéniz that he had been awarded the Croix de la Légion d'Honneur. Finally succumbing to Bright's disease, Albéniz died May 18, 1909 in Cambo-les-Bains in the French Pyrenees. Sent by train to Barcelona, he was buried in Cementiri de Sud-Oest on the seaward side of historic Montjuïc overlooking that famous city.

About the Music

España: Six Album Leaves, Op. 165 was composed around 1890 and published the same year. In this set of pieces, Albéniz magically transports the listener to colorful locations, each with its own special Spanish flavor. These attractive musical "postcards" are not particularly difficult technically, with a pedagogical level being somewhere between late intermediate and early advanced.

Albéniz created a new musical language for the piano, derived from Spain's heritage as found in its indigenous folk music. The interpretation of his music requires expressing a wide range of emotions—including joy, nostalgia, excitement, passion and sadness—all portrayed with subtle dynamic nuances. His music is often an impression of a landscape, event, or personal human experience. Performers must connect emotionally, but with artistic freedom and a confident spontaneity.

Spanish folk music evolved from four prominent cultures: Byzantine, Moorish, Gypsy and Jewish. During the Moorish occupation of Spain, there were musical and cultural influences that profoundly affected Spanish music. However, with the expulsion of the Moors in 1525, the lutes, bowed rebabs and tambourines used by the Moors were substituted for instruments favored by the Gypsies. With the guitar, castanets, muffled hand clapping and finger snapping, the Gypsies developed the *cante hondo* style, which became the popular *cante flamenco* of today.

Albéniz made changes of scenery a vital force in his personal life, as well as in his music. Three of the pieces in this set—*Prélude, Tango* and *Malagueña*—are representative of the southern region of Spain known as Andalucía, the area from which the composer frequently found creative inspiration. This is the land of *cante flamenco* and Gypsy folk music. Taking the guitar and castanets as his instrumental models, and incorporating poignant melodies and dazzling dance-like rhythms, Albéniz captures the very essence of this exciting music.

Albéniz combines varied stylistic elements in *España*. For example, in the *Serenata*, he contrasts the expressive melodic fragments of the *cante hondo* section with more rhythmic dance-like passages. The final two pieces, *Capricho Catalán* and *Zortzico* represent the north-east provinces of Catalonia and Basque, two regions of Spain whose people are renowned for their strong individualism. All of these pieces require subtle changes in tempo. Many of the ritardandos should be played as very slight rhythmic elongations, as if tempo rubato. Artistic pedaling—such as the use of half, quarter (or surface) depression, flutter pedal and una corda—allow for many different sonorities, and contribute to creating a mysterious, exotic ambience.

Performance Suggestions

No. 1, Prélude 6

This piece evokes Gypsy folk music. Its Arab-Andalusian influence includes use of the phrygian mode (with the lowered second step), used interchangeably with other pitch modifications. It is free in form, technically not demanding, and musically very rewarding. Create an intriguing, exotic mood by using visual imagery and imagination.

Compositionally, this piece uses stylistic elements of the Spanish idiom as found in the plaintively expressive melodic sections (measures 1–4). These phrases should be performed tempo rubato, alternating with the guitaristic passages (measures 5–8), which are performed in a more upbeat and steady tempo. At measures 17–28, the repeated triplet figures, simulating Spanish castanets, should be performed with absolute clarity and precision. In measure 34, lengthen the duration of the note on beat 2, creating an agogic accent for dramatic effect. At measures 46 and 48, the performer may explore the use of half pedal.

No. 2, Tango 10

One of Albéniz's well-known compositions, this popular dance is a model of refined elegance. The swaying rhythmic pattern in the bass cradles a charming melody. This magically creates a pleasant ambience for the music's message—a sentimentality both tender and nostalgic.

This piece employs rhythmic elements of the *habanera*, which is the ancestor of the Andalusian tango. Both are based on syncopated patterns within a $\frac{2}{4}$ meter. The melodic line should be voiced throughout the piece. Albéniz's frequent use of ritardando and ritenuto allows for a rhythmic freedom of expression more indicative of tempo rubato. These subtle tempo modifications are stylistically essential for an authentic interpretation.

No. 3, Malagueña

No. 3, Malagueña 13

Malagueña is the name of a popular song originating in the city of Málaga, made famous by Gypsy singers. This piece evokes the sound of flamenco music emanating from the small taverns found portside in Spain. Incorporating Gypsy folk elements, this piece includes aural images of dancers, guitars and castanets, and requires the sensitive interweaving of melody and accompaniment.

In ternary form, the A sections utilize both dance-like elements (measures 1 and 3) interspersed with instrumental elements, such as the triplet figurations that suggest castanets (measures 2 and 4). Play the triplets with clarity and precision. Measures 49–54 simulate a guitar, and should be performed with confidence and technical control. The B section (measures 64–84) is the *copla* (highly passionate refrain). Typically, Gypsies would draw out the melody to fulfill the music's emotional intent. Perform this section with flair and unrestrained emotion. The melodic exhortations in this section are interrupted by measures suggesting a guitar (measures 67, 71, etc.). In measure 148, the right hand notes "B" to "A" simulate the "Ay!" ending, typical of a Gypsy's anguished cry. Extend the duration of the "B" to create an agogic accent.

No. 4, Serenata

No. 4, Serenata 20

The music of this charming serenade features contrasting stylistic elements with sudden mood changes, ranging from *leggiero staccato* to an impassioned vocal declaration. Measures 1–8 suggest a dance, with measure 9 serving as an introduction to the singer. The repetitive single note in the bass at measures 5–8 provides a drum effect; this effect can also be found extensively throughout the B section. At measure 9 (and similar places), the phrases should be performed tempo rubato to allow for an expressive freedom. The B section (measures 41–76) retains the rhythm of a dance. Measure 109 is a brief coda containing Middle Eastern overtones in a *cante flamenco* style.

No. 5, Capricho Catalán

No. 5, Capricho Catalán 26

Albéniz was born in Catalonia and returned often to this region in northeast Spain. The word *capricho* connotes a pleasing, somewhat whimsical composition. In measures 3–54, be sure to shape the phrases to convey the beauty of the melodic line. During much of the piece, the right hand "sings" a happy song in harmonious thirds. All the while, the bass line produces a rotary rhythm—perhaps suggesting wagon wheels in motion—to accompany the pleasing melody. Albéniz found creative inspiration for his compositions from Spain's cultural heritage. Perhaps in this piece he is taking us on a *romería*, a traditional Spanish custom of that era, riding a horse-drawn carriage to the countryside for a picnic.

No. 6, Zortzico

No. 6, Zortzico 32

The paternal ancestral home of the Albéniz family is in the Alava area of the northern Basque region. A *zortzico* is a Basque folk dance in a lively $\frac{5}{8}$ meter, using dotted rhythms. This composition features repetitive notes resembling the colorful *tambour de Basque*, a small single-headed drum with hanging metal discs, similar to those on a tambourine. These metal discs produce a rhythmic sound that Albéniz cleverly captures in the quick sixteenth notes found throughout the piece.

The mood of this piece is exuberantly spirited! It requires shaping the musical phrases while maintaining a very steady beat in strict time. The piece is in ternary form, with the B section appearing at measure 35. The left hand assumes the melody at measures 35–37, then again at measure 43. Use your imagination to visualize young dancers in brightly colored costumes as they play their native instruments, representing their heritage with dignity and regional pride.

About This Edition

The location of the original manuscript for *España* is uncertain. Its opus number (Op. 165) is used in all editions, however it should be noted that all of Albéniz's opus numbers were carelessly assigned by him and his publishers. The details of the initial publication in 1890 are as follows: *España: Six Album Leaves*, Op. 165. London, W. Pitt & Hatzfeld; Boston, H. B. Stevens & Co.; collaborator editor, Louis H. Meyer, 1890. Printed in Leipzig, 1890.

This editor is indebted to Mr. Robert Balchin—curator of Music Collections in the British Library—for expediting the acquisition of a photocopy of the first 1890 printing, which served as the musical text for this edition. In addition to conducting research in the British Library, the editor consulted available editions of this work published in the United States and abroad. At the Académia Marshall in Barcelona, Spain, the editor studied with Alicia de Larrocha, who provided the Spanish legacy regarding the performance practice traditions of Albéniz's music.

Albéniz's works for the piano were his most inspired and original compositions, and have enjoyed universal appeal. However, his great talent did not include patient revision. *España* was initially published with many errors and omissions, which have been carried over into subsequent editions. Over the years, editors have produced new editions with some corrections, but little interpretive assistance. This edition not only contains numerous corrections, but also aids in interpretation through various additions in the score. The editor's main objective was to enlighten pianists to achieve an authentic and artistic interpretation, thereby preserving the performance practice traditions of Albéniz's music.

Editorial Considerations

All fingerings, phrase marks and pedal indications are editorial. Articulations and dynamics added by the editor were oftentimes placed in compliance with similar passages found elsewhere in the music. Additional editorial changes include: correction of inaccuracies in notation and rhythm; designation of *a tempo* after a ritardando or ritenuto; and redistribution of notes between the hands for technical and musical fluency. There are also suggested metronome marks as well as indications for subtle changes in tempo, which are integral to the stylistic performance of Spanish music.

Glossary of Spanish Terms

Andalucía—the southern region of Spain comprising the cities of Almería, Cádiz, Cordoba, Granada, Huelva, Jaén, Málaga and Sevilla. The region is known for its *cante flamenco* (see definition below).

cante hondo (cante jondo)—a melancholy song with repetition of short phrases, an absence of strict meter, expressive ornamentation and a tragic mood. It is often found in the middle section of ternary forms, or presented intermittently around dance-like passages.

cante flamenco—a song style developed from early 19th-century *cante hondo* with Middle Eastern influences. By the late 19th century, Gypsies adopted the *cante hondo*, renaming it *cante flamenco*.

copla—a stanza or refrain of the *cante hondo*. The Andalucían *copla* is the most highly passionate and intense.

flamenco—stylistic performances of folk songs and dances accompanied by guitars and castanets, particularly represented in southern Spain's Andalucían region.

malagueña—a popular flamenco song from Málaga made famous by singer Juan Breva (1844–1918).

zarzuela—a Spanish operetta with spoken dialogue, singing and dancing. It is named after La Zarzuela, the palace outside Madrid where, in the 17th century, comedians presented short programs before King Philip IV.

zortzico—folk music from the Basque region in the mountainous Pyrenees area of northern Spain. It is written in $\frac{5}{8}$ meter with frequent dotted rhythms.

ESPAÑA
Six Album Leaves

Prélude

Isaac Albéniz (1860–1909)
Op. 165

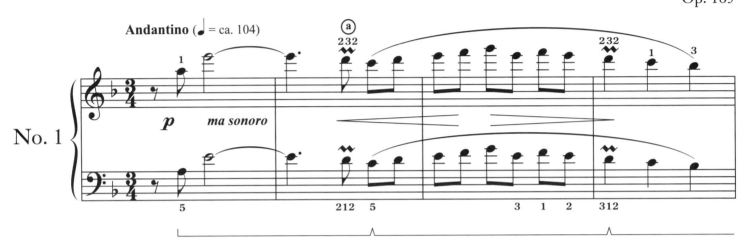

No. 1

Andantino (♩ = ca. 104)

p   *ma sonoro*

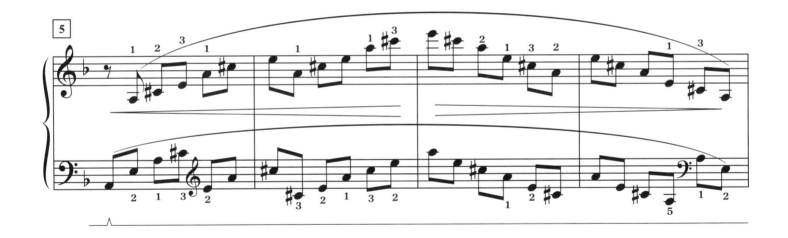

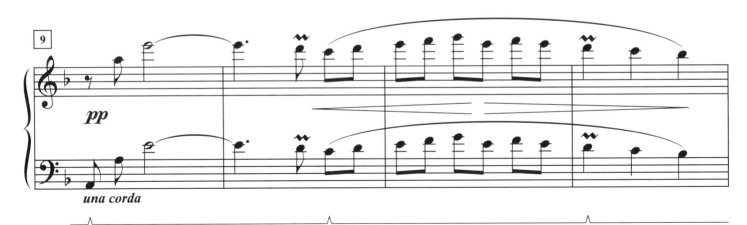

pp

una corda

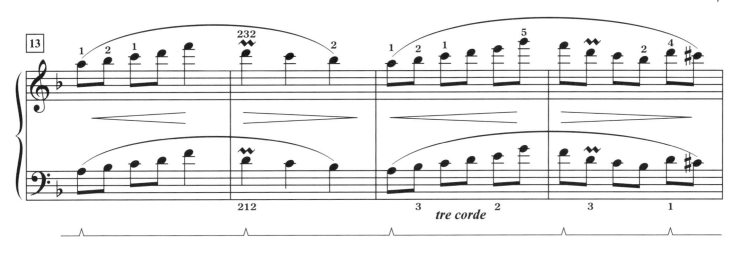

Tempo giusto

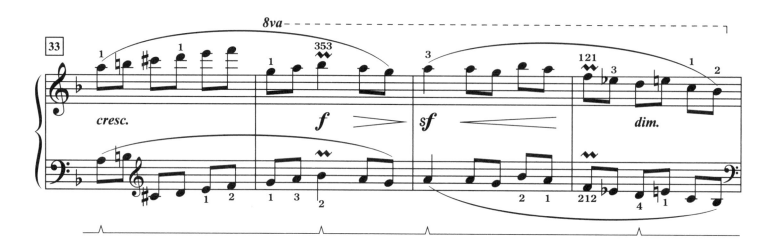

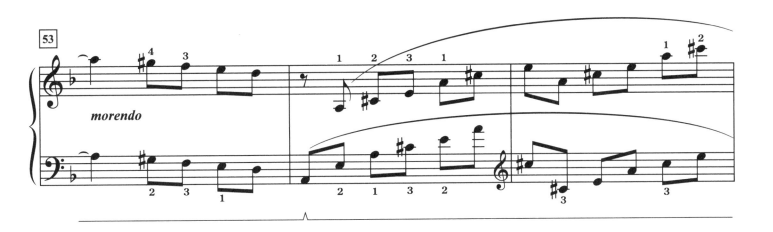

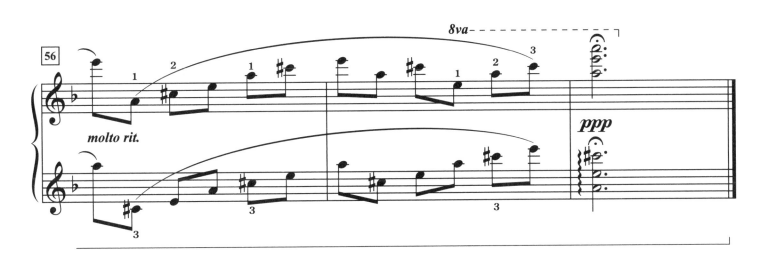

Tango

Malagueña

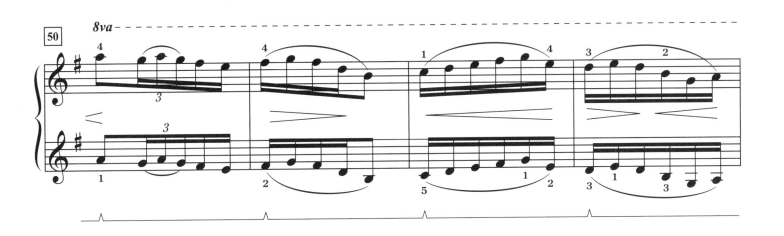

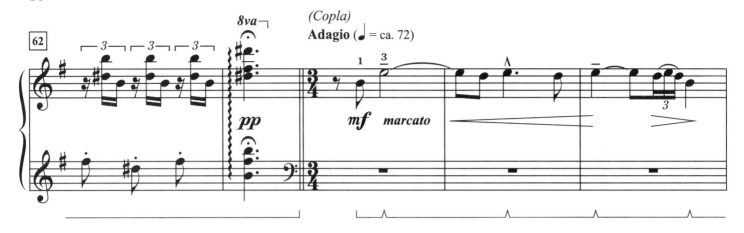

Serenata

No. 4

Capricho Catalán

No. 5

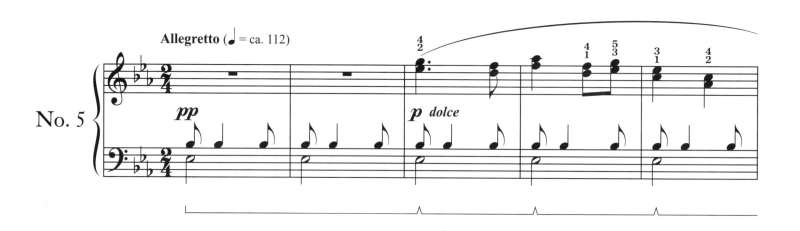

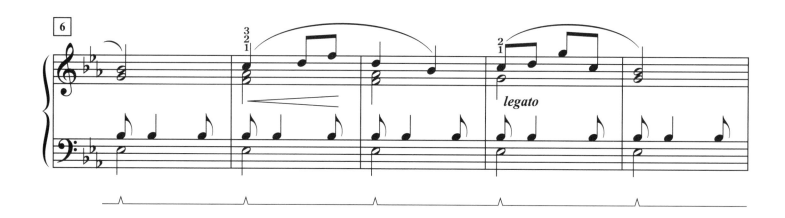

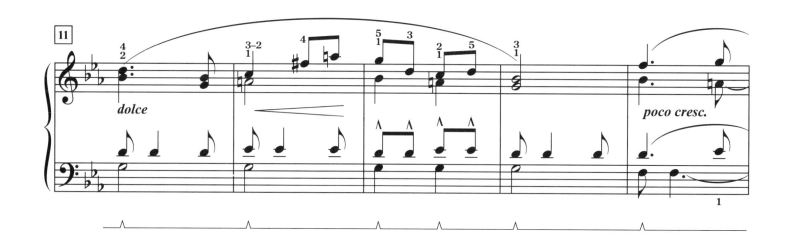

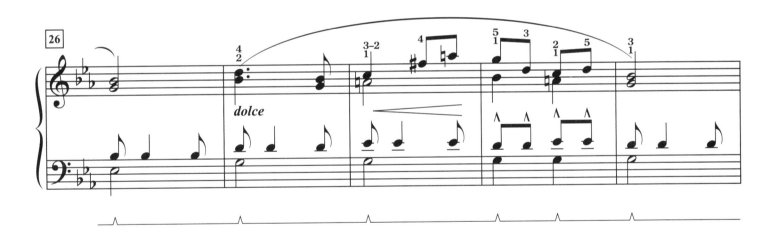

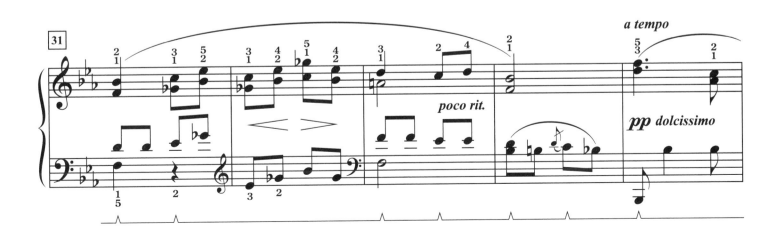

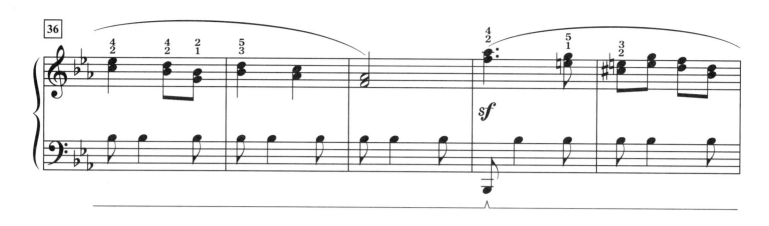

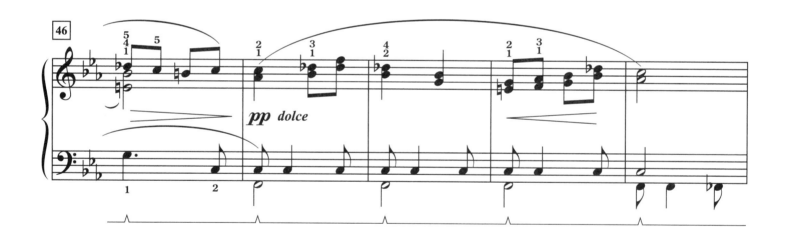

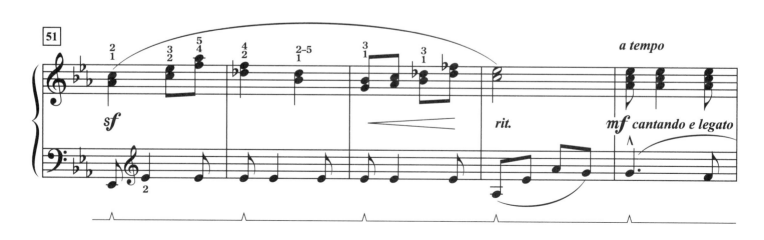

(a) Gradually release the pedal.

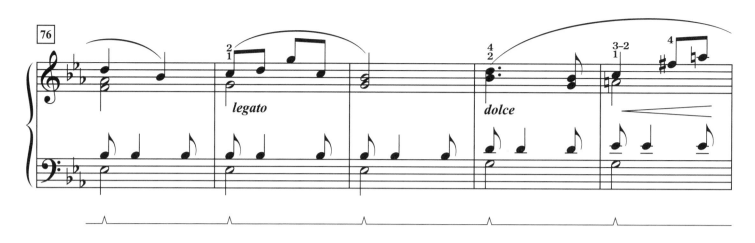

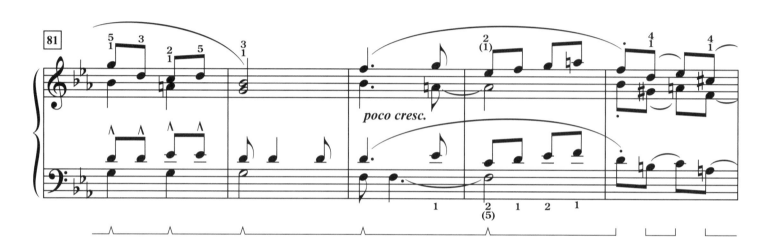

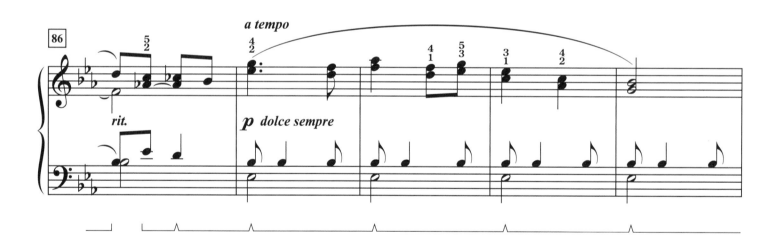

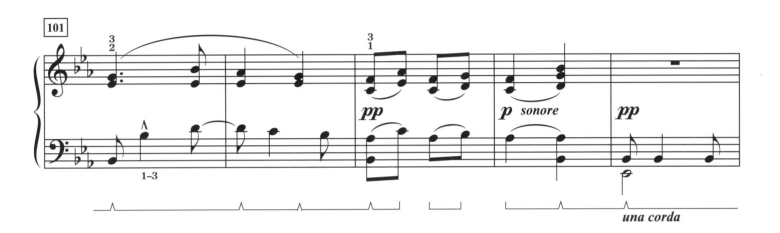

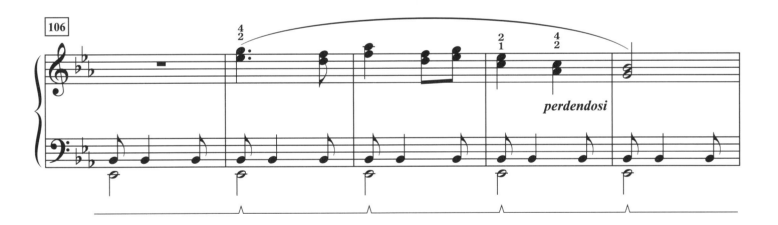

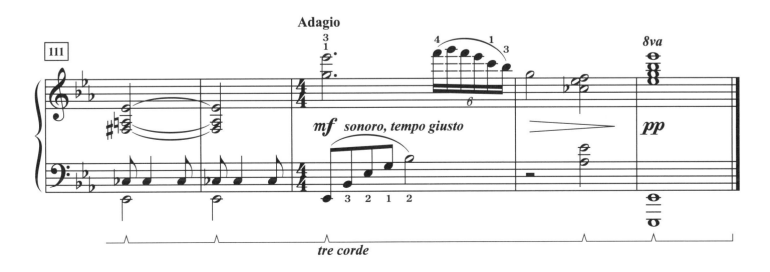

Zortzico

No. 6

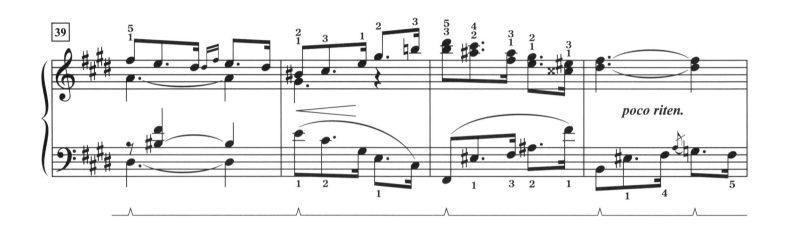

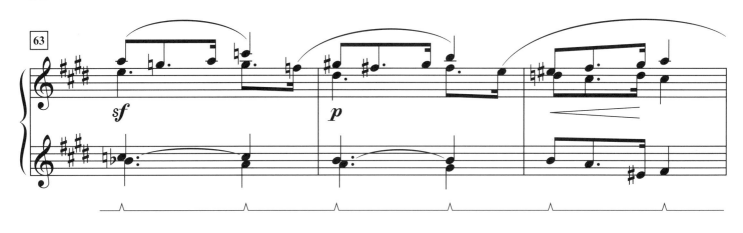

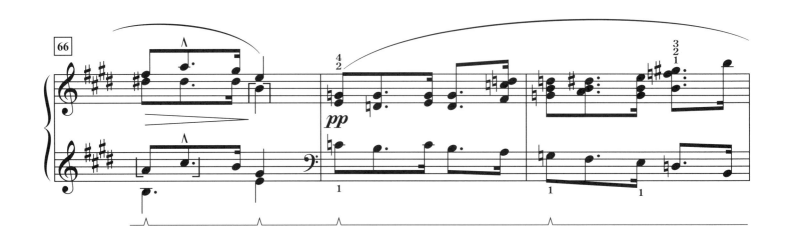

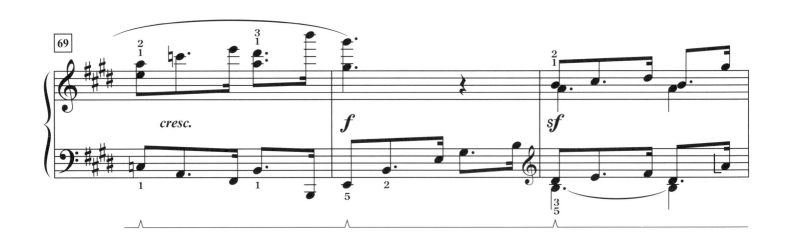

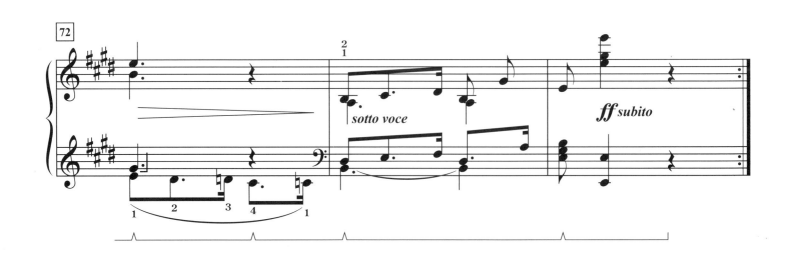